FROGS

by Michael Tyler

This edition first published in the United States in 1997 by
MONDO Publishing

By arrangement with MULTIMEDIA INTERNATIONAL (UK) LTD

The publisher would like to thank Densey Clyne, Mantis Wildlife, for her assistance.

Diagrams by Lynn Twelftree

Photograph Credits: Schafer & Hill/Tony Stone Images: front cover; Murray Littlejohn: pp. 4, 14 left, 16 left, 18; Margaret Davies: p. 6; Densey Clyne: pp. 7, 9 top, 10 right, 11 top, 12, 14 right, 15, 16 right, 19, 23, 24; Queensland Museum: pp. 8-9 burrowing sequence; Bohdan Stankewytsch-Janusch: pp. 10 left, 13; Jim Frazier: pp. 11 bottom, 20; Fred Parker: p. 25; Dale Caville: p. 26.

For information contact:
MONDO Publishing
980 Avenue of the Americas
New York, NY 10018

Printed in Hong Kong
First Mondo printing, October 1996
01 02 03 04 05   9 8 7 6 5

Originally published in Australia in 1987 by Horwitz Publications Pty Ltd
Original development by Robert Andersen & Associates and Snowball Educational
Cover redesign by Charlotte Staub

          Library of Congress Cataloging-in-Publication Data

Tyler, Michael J.
     Frogs / by Michael Tyler.
        p.   cm. — (Mondo animals)
     Includes index.
     Summary: Discusses types and physical features of frogs, their calls, life
cycles, what they eat, how to care for tadpoles, and more.
        ISBN 1-57255-191-7 (pbk. : alk. paper)
        1. Frogs—Juvenile literature. [1. Frogs.] I. Title. II. Series.
     QL668.E2T94   1996
     597.8—dc20   96-15297
                                               CIP
                                               AC

Cover: Pair of Ornate Horned Frogs

Types of frogs

So far more than 4000 different species of frogs have been found in the world and scientists believe that others will be discovered. There are 88 different species in the United States and Canada. At least 208 different species of frogs have been discovered in Australia.

Scientists divide frogs into a number of groups called families. The frogs are grouped according to the way they look and the way they live.

Tree frogs are found in many countries and belong to one family. They usually live in trees and bushes. They have sticky discs on the tips of their fingers and toes to help them climb on smooth leaves and branches.

Types of frogs

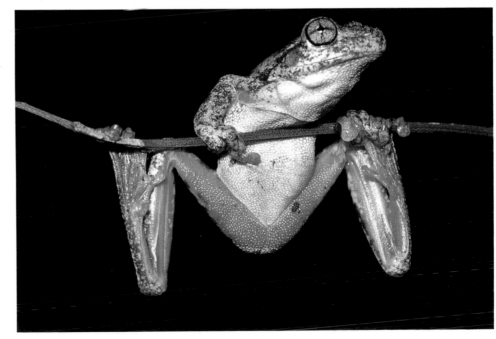

Land and water frogs are found worldwide and belong to many different families. These frogs are found in all kinds of places, including rainforests and deserts. They live in the water, or on the ground, or in burrows.

Many of the desert frogs burrow with the help of a spade-like projection on each foot.

Sequence of photographs showing desert frog burrowing

8 Types of frogs

Rainforest frog (left)

Features of frogs

Frogs vary in size. The largest frog in the world, *Conraua goliath* in West Africa, is about 12 inches (300 mm) long. The smallest frog, *Sminthillus limbatus* in Cuba, is ½ inch (12 mm). One of the largest frogs in the United States, the bullfrog, is 3½–6 inches (88–150 mm) long, and the smallest is the little grass frog, ⅝ inch (16 mm) long.

The smallest frog in Australia (above)

The largest frog in Australia (right)

Scale drawing showing difference in size between these two species (left)

All frogs are similar in important ways.

They have smooth skin which must be kept moist. For this reason they always live in or near damp places.

Desert habitat where frogs keep moist by living underground until it rains (right)

Habitat with natural springs where tree, land and water frogs live (bottom left)

Dam near Snowy Mountains where tree and land frogs live (bottom right)

Frogs' eyes and nostrils are on top of their heads so that they are able to see and breathe while the rest of the body is under water.

Most frogs are excellent swimmers. Some kick with their strong back legs but others use a dog-paddle style.

Features of frogs

Frogs have short arms and long legs to help them leap. A species of frog in South Africa holds the world record for leaping: 34 feet (10.3 meters) in three leaps.

The rocket frog is found in eastern and northern Australia. It is known to jump long distances

13

Most frogs are green or brown and are hard to see. The Australian corroboree frog, with its bright colors, seems to stand out, but it also blends in with its surroundings.

A common brown frog (above)

Australian corroboree frog (right)

Features of frogs

Frogs and toads

Toads have warty skin, stout bodies and short legs. They crawl and hop rather than leap. Because some Australian frogs look like toads they have been called toads or toadlets. However, the only true toad found in Australia is the cane toad which was introduced to control sugar cane beetles. Toads are often poisonous.

Cane toad

Frog calls

Frogs make a variety of calls for different reasons. During breeding time the male makes a call to attract females. This call also tells other males that the territory is now occupied. Each species of frog has its own call and to make the sound louder the male blows up his throat. Male and female frogs also give a high-pitched scream or a series of chirrups if they are distressed, and a grunt or squawk as a warning sound.

The life cycle of frogs

The life cycle of frogs and the development of the young varies from one species to another. The following describes the life cycle of one common frog.

During breeding time, the male frog goes to the breeding place and calls mostly at night.

The female comes to the breeding place and lays many eggs. This may take several hours. While laying eggs the female raises her hands just above the surface of the water and throws them down, creating air bubbles. Behind her the male pours his fertilizing fluid over the eggs. Frogs' eggs are coated with a jelly which protects them. Some frogs lay as many as 25,000 eggs at a time while others lay only 20.

The life cycle of frogs

Marsh frogs laying and fertilizing eggs (left)

Marsh frog spawn (above)

The eggs slowly develop into tadpoles over a period of a few days. When the tadpoles are ready to escape from the jelly they wriggle and break out through the jelly wall.

While they are growing, tadpoles spend all of their time feeding. At this stage of development they have many rows of teeth, which they use to scrape food from stems and rocks or from the bottom of the pond. Later they may feed on insects and other small creatures in the water.

Inside a tadpole's mouth

teeth

horny beak

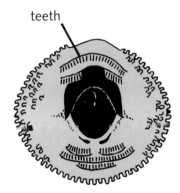

Peron's tree frog tadpole

giant burrowing frog tadpole

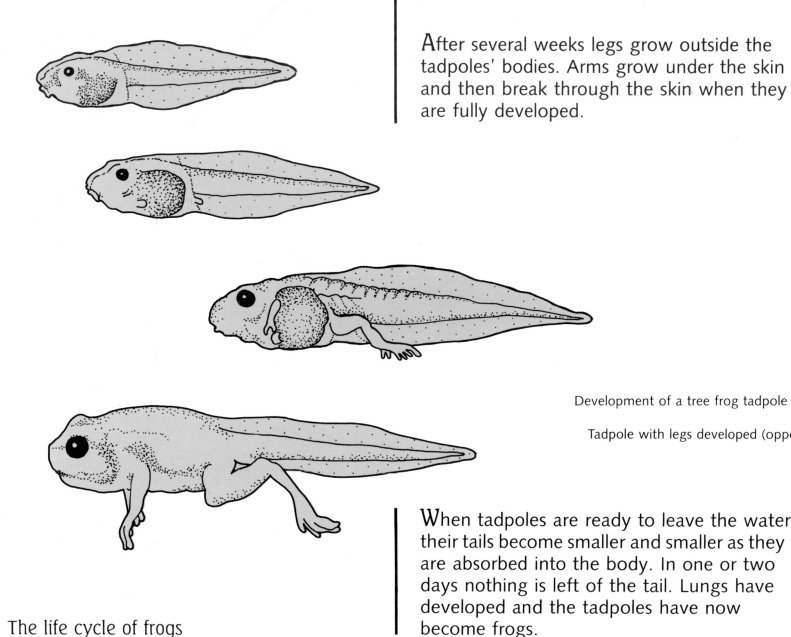

After several weeks legs grow outside the tadpoles' bodies. Arms grow under the skin and then break through the skin when they are fully developed.

Development of a tree frog tadpole (left)

Tadpole with legs developed (opposite)

When tadpoles are ready to leave the water their tails become smaller and smaller as they are absorbed into the body. In one or two days nothing is left of the tail. Lungs have developed and the tadpoles have now become frogs.

The life cycle of frogs

Some frogs do not lay their eggs in water. They lay them in little nests on moist ground so that the eggs do not dry out and there is enough water for the tadpoles to begin to grow in their jelly capsules. When heavy rain falls the tadpoles are washed into a pond where they complete their growth.

The life cycle of frogs

The tadpoles of some species stay inside their capsules until they reach the frog stage. The eggs of these species need to be laid on very moist ground and the capsules need to be strong to withstand the kicking of the babies as they grow.

Developing tadpole shown without its protective capsule

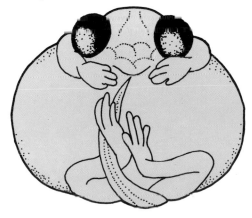

The stomach brooding frog has a most unusual life cycle. The female swallows her eggs or young tadpoles and keeps them in her stomach. The tadpoles produce a chemical to stop the stomach from making acid so that they are not digested. When the tadpoles have developed into little frogs they are born through the mother's mouth.

How tadpoles and frogs breathe

When frogs are at the tadpole stage they can breathe under water because they have gills. Adult frogs breathe with lungs, as humans do, but they also breathe through their skin, getting oxygen from the air or water. To be able to breathe through their skin frogs must keep the skin moist. They also breathe through the roofs of their mouths.

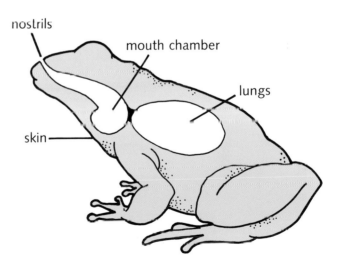

nostrils

mouth chamber

lungs

skin

What frogs eat

Frogs eat insects, snails and other small creatures including other frogs! To catch insects they flick out their long, sticky tongues onto their prey. They then flick their tongues back into their mouths. The food is not chewed even though some frogs have teeth.

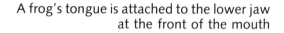

A frog's tongue is attached to the lower jaw at the front of the mouth

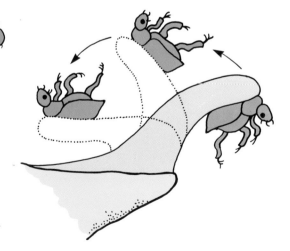

Caring
for
tadpoles

The time to collect eggs or tadpoles is in the early spring or summer.

A good home for tadpoles is a large bowl, a plastic bucket, or (best of all) a glass aquarium.

It is best to use water from the pond, dam or creek where you have collected the eggs or tadpoles. Tap water contains chlorine which kills tadpoles. To rid tap water of chlorine, let it stand in a bucket for 24 hours before using it.

Keep only a few tadpoles in one container and change the water when it gets dirty.

The best food for tadpoles is lettuce leaves which have been boiled until they are limp, or dried, tropical fish food. Make sure there is always just enough food in the aquarium and that you cover the top of the container with wire or cloth so that the froglets do not jump out. Without water, the froglets cannot survive.

When their arms are starting to appear provide a raft or bench onto which the froglets can climb or rest.

Return the baby frogs to their original environment.

Caring for tadpoles

Disappearing frogs

Since 1980 many kinds of frogs have vanished. Even the wonderful stomach breeding frog (p. 26) has become extinct.

Scientists believe that pollution and disease are the main causes for the loss.

You can help by caring for the ponds and creeks where frogs live and breed. Clean up your local pond by taking out any trash or litter. Encourage your friends to help make the environment clean and healthy.

Index

Frogs depicted in this book

PAGE

4 *Litoria burrowsae*, Burrow's tree frog
6 *Litoria peroni*, Peron's tree frog
7 *Litoria gracilenta*, slender tree frog (top left)
   Litoria aurea, green and golden bell frog (top right)
   Litoria peroni, Peron's tree frog (bottom right)
8 & 9 *Notaden bennetti*, crucifix toad (shown burrowing)
9 *Cophixalus ornatus*, ornate frog (top)
10 *Litoria microbelos*, javelin frog (left)
   Litoria infrafrenata, white-lipped tree frog (right)
12 *Limnodynastes terraereginae*, northern banjo frog (top)
   Adelotus brevis, tusked frog (bottom)
13 *Litoria nasuta*, rocket frog
14 *Mixophyes balbus*, stuttering frog (left)
   Pseudophryne corroboree, corroboree frog (right)
15 *Bufo marinus*, cane toad
16 *Limnodynastes tasmaniensis*, spotted grass frog (left)
   Limnodynastes peroni, brown marsh frog (right)
18 *Limnodynastes interioris*, giant banjo frog
19 *Limnodynastes peroni*, brown marsh frog (left)
24 Eggs of *Geocrinia victoriana*, eastern smooth frog
25 Eggs and newly-hatched froglet of *Discodeles* (right)
26 *Rheobatrachus silus*, stomach brooding frog

Habitats depicted in this book

PAGE

11 Outback, Kinchega National Park, NSW, Australia (top right)
   Natural Springs, Mataranka Springs, NT, Australia (bottom left)
   Dam near Eucumbene, Snowy Mountains, NSW, Australia (bottom right)